CSU Poetry Series XXIX

Thylias Moss

At Redbones

Cleveland State University Poetry Center

ACKNOWLEDGMENTS

Grateful acknowledgment is made to the following periodicals in which some of these poems originally appeared:

CALLALOO: "The Root of the Road," "To Buckwheat and Other Pickaninnies"

EPOCH: "Washing Bread"

FIELD: "A Godiva"

GARGOYLE: "Lunchcounter Freedom"

GRAHAM HOUSE REVIEW: "November and Aunt Jemima," "Spilled Sugar"

IOWA REVIEW: "Fullness," "Redbones as Nothing Special," "She's Florida Missouri But Was Born in Valhermosa and Lives in Ohio"

PLOUGHSHARES: "She Did My Hair Outside, the Wash a Tent Around Us"

Thanks to the National Endowment for the Arts and the Kenan Charitable Trust for grants which allowed some of these poems to be written.

ISBN 0-914946-73-0

Funded Through
Ohio Arts Council

727 East Main Street
Columbus, Ohio 43205-1796
(614) 466-2613

CONTENTS

This book is dedicated
to the memory of Calvin Theodore Brasier
and to his memories of Frizell Brasier

At Redbones

FULLNESS

One day your place in line will mean the
Eucharist has run out. All because you waited
your turn. Christ's body can be cut into only
so many pieces. One day Jesus will be eaten up.
The Last Supper won't be misnamed. One day the
father will place shavings of his own blessed fingers
on your tongue and you will get back in line for
more. You will not find yourself out of line again.
The bread will rise inside you. A loaf of tongue.
Pumpernickel liver. You will be the miracle.
You will feed yourself five thousand times.

LUNCHCOUNTER FREEDOM

I once wanted a white man's eyes upon
me, my beauty riveting him to my slum
color. Forgetting his hands are made for my
curves, he would raise them to shield his eyes
and they would fly to my breasts with gentleness
stolen from doves.

I've made up my mind not to order a sandwich on
light bread if the waitress approaches me
with a pencil. My hat is the one I wear
the Sundays my choir doesn't sing. A dark
bird on it darkly sways to the gospel music,
trying to pull nectar from a cloth flower.
Psalms are mice in my mind, nibbling,
gnawing, tearing up my thoughts.
White men are the walls. I can't tell anyone
how badly I want water. In the mirage that
follows, the doves unfold into hammers.
They still fly to my breasts.

Because I'm nonviolent I don't act or
react. When knocked from the stool
my body takes its shape from what
it falls into. The white man cradles
his tar baby. Each magus in turn.
He fathered it, it looks just like him,
the spitting image. He can't let go of
his future. The menu offers tuna fish,
grits, beef in a sauce like desire.
He is free to choose from available
choices. An asterisk marks the special.

PROVOLONE BABY

She threw the baby out with the bath water. He was part
of what made her dirty. In the shower she sang songs
other people had written. She uprooted the flowers on
her wallpaper. The living room looked like Swiss cheese.
She prefers provolone because she sings what others
write and the baby gets dirty all the time inside her. Dirt
originates inside. Volcanoes never spew out anything
clean just Swiss cheese, babies, lava corsages that she
won't wear because his promises were songs other
people had written about gin which she threw out
because it was bath water and she was through bathing
his forehead with isopropyl to bring him back to a time
of flowers and composition when he didn't smell like a
volcano but like a baby that never got dirty, that never
took root inside her, whose bath water she could cook in
although she wasn't a good cook, she was used to
throwing things away, the delicious going bad as if
throwing a tantrum and ruining the walls so she throws
them out, she peels her house, strips away all the dirty
layers to a provolone baby that needs a bath. *Ooh Baby,*
she sings, *ooh Baby, you make me feel so good,* she sings
because that's how the song was written, the way it's
supposed to go. The words ride suds down the drain,
shampoo blossoms melt down her back.

PARADE OF UMBRELLAS

Umbrellas are held in a way that only they and
legs can be seen. At first this seems reasonable.
New York where in just walking to the subway
everyone auditions for the Rockettes.

And you do like seeing drops slide down taut
nylon like nightgowns down hairless legs.

Then you think about the way they protect themselves
from water, you wonder if they shower, bathe, are
baptized.

You look for someone to join you, run without
a shield, prove that the sky is firing blanks
just like in the movies.

I use an umbrella when my parents curse.
They always do when I'm
not at the movies.

EUCHARISTIC OPTIONS

Wherever there are shadows there
is Thomas jugging his hands into

wounds. One thing Jesus could not do
was sin. His was a divine repertoire.

When Thomas proved Jesus bled
like a man, he

established Eucharistic options: bathing
with menstruating women bloodying the

baptismal river, biting stigmata into
lactating breasts to add ruddy honey to

the milk, or stabbing strangers to
start the fountain.

BAKING THE EUCHARIST

Whatever is in your hands goes
into the dough, the frustration wiped
off the brow, the desire to
slap, the doubt of hands whose
applause is indecisiveness
about prayer.

This then is the therapy of
making bread. Eating it
makes therapy necessary.

A CATCHER FOR AN ATOMIC BOUQUET

I have just watched Eyes on the Prize
twenty years after the contest. I am looking
at my winnings: a husband who is not literary, a
baby from a teen-ager's body, a daughter from
a sister-in-law declared unfit.
I've had both kinds of abortions, the
voluntary, the involuntary. Stop. This
personal maze is not the prize. Stop. Writers,
my class believes, must write about what they
know, restrict themselves to expertise.
That rule leaves me no province.

I have played that game to toss a quarter
into a milk bottle with a hymen. I left the
kiosk, stuffed flamingos and Saint Bernards
still suspended from the ceiling like plucked
chickens, ducks, onions, eels at a Hangzhou
outdoor market.

When the baby tugs at me he is no prize; a prize
just doesn't force its acceptance. You could
easily look at him thinking how you didn't bring
him into the world, he isn't really your
responsibility. You just signed your name on
a sheaf of paper that could have been one of the
usual bad checks. You know, however, who's doing
all the insisting that the baby stay in the world.
Who's loving the insistence. Insistence is the prize.
The faces of Hiroshima stayed on the walls, apocalyptic
posters. No one caught the bouquet thrown at the
nuclear wedding. Exploding flowers as from a joke
shop. I've got my eyes on the flamingo withdrawing
at least one leg he insists won't be shit on.

NOVEMBER AND AUNT JEMIMA

We sit at the table and that is grace,
the way one commits the prelude to kowtowing
by folding into the chair.

Usually we eat as if on a subway,
among strangers, standing to avoid the
toilet seat. Today, though, is Thanksgiving

so guilt bibs us, an extra place
is set for Aunt Jemima, the pancake box
occupies the chair, the family resemblance

unmistakeable. Hips full as Southern Baptist
tents but of a different doctrine.
Teeth white as the shock of lynching, thirty-two

tombstones. Despite the headrag
neither she nor her sister that bore me
are mistaken for gypsies.

The color of corrosion, she is not called
classic. The syrup that is the liquid
version of her skin flows like the promised

milk and honey so once a year we welcome
her. Even Christ would not be welcome every
day. Especially Christ who cannot come

without judgment just as she cannot come
without pancakes, flat, humane stones
still thrown at her by those whose sins

being white are invisible as her pain, the
mix in the box after the grinding of bones.

THE ADVERSARY

I understand God's reasons for keeping
Satan to himself, the only rabbit caught
on a tiring eternal hunt. Who wouldn't want
to go a few rounds with the devil that made
one of us paint a moustache on the Virgin,
increasing the likelihood that she stay one?
Imagine having to be famous for what she never had.
She can't go a few rounds with him anyway,
being unable to afford losing all she's got,
that cat's eye virginity that has to undergo
nine immaculate lifetimes before the fad dies and
we don't care what's inside her other than transplantable
organs. We'd tear him apart if God let us.

I can't forget that God's a man, subject to
the quirks of maleness, among them that need
for adversary, for worthy opponent, for just short
of equal. And that's Satan, the runner up, the
one who almost had it all, a do-nothing second in command.
The smell of victory roses mutes his protest. The consolation
of smelling them too he takes home.

Think of it, his authority denied him by a nose, a
longer, pointier Caucasian nose. And Satan is there
for God no matter what, the original Uncle Tom.

To be the winner, God needs a run for the money, a sprinter
in the next lane with the potential to grab the gold yet
who defers, won't cross the line without more information
about the other side, without a taster, a patsy
for the poison.

FOR THOSE WHO CAN'T PEEL THE POTATOES CLOSE ENOUGH

1.
Blondell, who engraved Bridgett's face with my nails,
looks cherubic in photos from my five-candle party.
She wasn't invited, no one thirteen was. Because she was
there in bluish skin, because she wasn't a selfish breather
she became my babysitter. Sometimes the only payment she'd
accept was three White Castle burgers.
With my eyes closed I still see her popping my buttons,
offering a choice of rapist, the knife or her younger brother.
The night before Bridgett went back to Milwaukee
Blondell bound her in the basement with the choice of
     heated
flat iron to kiss or either of Blondell's two sets of lips.

The point is Blondell's courtesy. Her earned position
as legend. Her thank-you when her brother turned to zip
and cry.

2.
When Jesus was thirty-three
he began his work for the kingdom,
scorpions tasted his heels,
he crossed the desert in a mirage,
walking to his death as to a
lost brother.
He always knelt on his shadow.
Now I am thirty-three
and sometimes unable to feel my right leg,
a numbness that threatened my pelvis
and my ability to feel what has been
the best part of marriage,
a numbness first felt in a restaurant,
biting through fried haddock

and my lower lip
until blood spurted and I stopped at red
as I always do.
A red carpet is a tongue of blood.
Jesus never married.
I never French kiss.

3.
My son is called Dennis
after my lawless brother-in-law
after Blondell's brother.
He completes an anti-trinity.

4.
Mrs. Arnstein doesn't know I listened
to her in the middle of the night.
With my fingers in my ears I housed
her crying in my head.
Together we watched smoke rising over
the harbor. "That's him," she said.
The Aryan woman on the Blue Bonnet box
is as excited about oleo as I would be
about ceasefire. Mrs. Arnstein needs
a rest from the past.

5.
Skylines graph rising courtesy
and are shrines to her. The story of
her sainthood is the story of the stone
at the foot of a beach, washed daily,
gleaming as with holy oil when
the water recedes
as the Red Sea did
as the flood did
skeletons in their wake.
Medusa that Blondell was, she knew better

than to look at herself so her transformation
to stone leads me to conclude the miraculous
visited. Blessed rock, holy rock, a definitive
prayer. I can put my faith in such objects.
See, I throw one
and Blondell walks on water
before she drowns.

6.
All this is to show how we
are not a godless nation. Those who can't
peel the potatoes close enough are not
doomed. Look around. Some beaten women stay
in love because Jesus stayed on the cross.
The rhythm of belts finds a refrain in church
bells. Monastic silences govern many marriages.
A jackhammer makes a pentecostal call to
worship. Tough saints like Blondell beat us
into submission, into clay God can use to
reshape us. The method of salvation doesn't
matter. Let us receive the gun's sacrament, bullets
made of petrified bits of two-thousand-year-old body
followed by the siren's benediction.

SPILLED SUGAR

I cannot forget the sugar on the table.
The hand that spilled it was not that of
my usual father, three layers of clothes
for a wind he felt from hallway to kitchen,
the brightest room though the lightbulbs
were greasy.

The sugar like bleached anthills of ground teeth.
It seemed to issue from open wounds in his palms.
Each day, more of Father granulated, the injury spread
like dye through cotton, staining all the wash,
condemning the house.

The gas jets on the stove shoot a blue spear
that passes my cheek like air. I stir
and the sugar dissolves, the coffee giving no evidence
that it has been sweetened and I will not taste it
to find out, my father raised to my lips, the toast burnt,
the breakfast ruined.

Neither he nor I will move from the shrine
of Mother's photo. We begin to understand
the limits of love's power. And as we do,
we have to redefine God; he is not love at all.
He is longing.

He is what he became those three days
that one third of himself was dead.

THE EYELID'S STRUGGLE

We watch the pigeons bring back
the crusts left on the curb, the stiff
contexts for rye centers. If news
were history we would still read the paper.
History tells us what is worth remembering.
Not Mother's postage-stamp sized obituary.
Grief for her would be wasted, she
did not start a war, she did not stop one.
She patted on powder two shades lighter than
her face, an inch of white lies that
rubbed off on her pillow. The lies
would not stay buried. White lies
are history, white lies are policy, broken
promises to Indians.

We need to know what happened
to the canteen that formed the base
of the lamp that vanished when
I turned it off. I couldn't find
the switch in the dark; I felt like a blind
woman choosing tomatoes and realized absence
of sight did not mean absence of prejudice.
Absence of prejudice is a white lie. Mother
wore absence of prejudice to bed, when
Father kissed her, it was on his lips.
The canteen used to hold water but we didn't thirst
in the daytime. We needed light more than water.
Overnight, though, dry dreams delivered dehydration,
soda cracker clouds cracked into Communion that
cut our tongues; that was the blood, not symbolic
wine; that was salvation, the scar tissue that
formed stops us from lying.

At my request he stopped calling me rabbit.
After that, batches of his hot slaw traveled
like lava from the kitchen. It seasoned
everything, made it taste the same.
It brought the absence of prejudice to
the palate, it burned the tastebuds, we ate
hell to eliminate it as an outcome. Above
our heads the cooing suggested immature lambs,
incomplete sacrifice. The flapping
was the eyelid's struggle with tears.
When one must learn about life from a
pigeon, one learns what hardened the crusts
in the first place. A dead rabbit
doesn't always mean new life will enter the
world, sometimes just
that something is gone, won't ever
be back, that you have killed.

THE ROOT OF THE ROAD

My hem eats the dirt haunting
my footsteps with apparitions of flies.
The road is a tongue stretched speechless.
Where I trampled faceless, I would be this
road. Whenever possible I look for where
the mouth was, I lament its loss of hair, the
uselessness of my toes combing the dirt like
plows. My own hair hangs like old udders.
I am the milk by-pass, the shortcut to hunger.

Mistress Jane, color of dough, twisted into fancy
bread, yeasty, floury, my hands when I bathe her.
She is not the one whose rising proclaims day.
She wants the road to Natchez when she looks at me,
my back doesn't disappoint. I don't feel her hand
when it touches my shoulder to guide it. What is
on me couldn't make itself felt though I wore it all
day like an epaulet. Even after removing my calico,
her glove, a layer of air prevailed, separating our skin.

My hands circled her neck following the road's
curve. Dust flew from her mouth disguised as
breath. Had she stayed mute she would have lived,
those words *after all I've done for you* (said also
to her mirror) buried me while I held onto her.
The displaced dirt from the hastily dug grave went
on walking the parent road as me. Mistress Jane was
quite comfortable underground with other roots.
Who besides the flies will believe I held a pink flower
by its pinker stem.

HATTIE AND THE POWER OF BISCUITS

This one is about dignity, they all
are. Hattie was an awful big
maid. Her cannon shape was appropriate
for what came out of her. She
gave context to *Gone with the Wind*, she
is what outlived Tara in significance.

In 1939 she received her Oscar for
the best supporting role, the best job
holding up the confederacy, nourishing the
nation, the white family she was *like* a
member of without being tucked into a goose-
down bed or appearing in the albums brought out
on holidays. Hers was the power of biscuits.
What a wonder she didn't use strychnine dough.
Hers was the power of the backdoor key, the
privilege to see how they really live. What
a way to start believing in yourself, to know
you don't ever want to be white. Hattie had
her bones dyed.

Biscuits cut from her cheeks by household
pinches that today reset circuit breakers in
overloaded homes. She worked so hard
the effort churned her salty milk, babies
raised on cheesiness and butter, able to siphon
anything through a straw.

THE ECLIPSE AND THE HOLY MAN

The many-paned window in a cold
room made me see the winding oak in
sections. One consists wholly of old
fingers whose sensing the weight of air
inspires attempts to grasp it. One
part's bend is analogous to the holy man's
shoulders. He rises out of nowhere as he
walks up the hill. He is dressed like an
eclipse, a revival of light in tandem.

Where the window ends, the oak becomes
blue plaster, impenetrable sky that injures
faith. When birds drop accent them as
answers to prayers or there will be none.
Birds of prey aren't holy. Congregations
of pigeons aren't having church though they eat
the holy man's bread. The sign of the cross
is a deaf communication the hearing may ignore.

Maybe eagles can't fly anymore but watch
them somersault when I flip coins. The heads,
the tails don't help make up my mind about
what to believe. Flipping them was just easy judo.

When the holy man walks away, the eclipse is
total. One cannot prove the sun exists.

RAISING A HUMID FLAG

Enough women over thirty are at Redbones for
the smell of Dixie Peach to translate the air.
I drink when I'm there because you must have
some transparency in this life and you can't see
through the glass till it's empty. Of course I get
next to men with broad feet and bull nostrils to
ward off isolation. You go to Redbones after
you've been everywhere else and can see the rainbow
as fraud, a colorful frown.
The best part is after midnight when the crowd
at its thickest raises a humid flag and hotcombed
hair reverts to nappy origins. I go to Redbones to
put an end to denial. Dixie Peach is a heavy pomade
like canned-ham gelatin. As it drips down foreheads
and necks, it's like tallow dripping down candles
in sacred places.

THOSE MEN AT REDBONES

Those men at Redbones who call me Mama don't
want milk.

They are lucky. A drop of mine
is like a bullet. You can tell
when a boy has been raised on ammunition,
his head sprouts wire. All
those barbed afros.

Those men at Redbones who call me Mama want
to repossess.

One after the other they try
to go back where they came from.
Only the snake
has not outgrown the garden.

WASHING BREAD

In the river a woman washes bread, big
white slices
like shirts.
When she wrings them, milky water
runs from wrists to elbows
and she remembers the loaf swelling,
pronouncing starvation.
When she lays the bread on nearby
rocks she is a nurse swabbing fever.
It dries and gets dirty again.
Her children eat pieces
of their crosses.

LOOKING FOR LAZARUS

My daughter has not been home since the myrtle
bloomed. She went looking for her brother
and didn't return. I know her, she looked
in chimneys, in alleys, dark places
where you can't be sure you didn't see
what can't be seen in lighted rooms even
when the lamp is the eye.

She has no brother, Cain said that too, but I
would know if twice my body had emptied itself.

The chimney's tight squeeze is like being
with a man I can say because I've been
with one before. My daughter has not, she
must have thought she was in another birth
canal, another tunnel of love and was reborn
to someone else.

She knew Christians could be born again
and again but not, she didn't know, if
they really died.

A magician doesn't reveal his tricks, his God,
his illusion, and the volunteer from the audience,
if others are to believe, takes part, becomes a
savior, stops believing.

DEATH OF THE SWEET WORLD

People are going to think my mother
is dead. I write about her as if she'd died
because she will. My preparation is more
necessary than morbid. She'll want me
to style her hair, touch the embalmed
cheek, slip a ring my father meant to buy
on her finger.

What will happen to the rooms
she used to clean, the wealthy widows
who asked her to iron wrinkle-free linens
and had tables set for two, coffee steaming
when she arrived? I used to tell her to get
a decent job.

Her heavy perfume scented the early morning
like olfactory fog. The bags
she carried to the bus stop made her
look homeless. She was in charge
of all the church's books except the Bible.

She didn't understand that Hungary
was a country yet knew people lived there.
When she said grace her hands swept
across the meal as if she was in love with
the broom. Now she can't eat salt or sugar,
the sweet world is gone, the sour and bitter
remain.

Life alone does not impress me. The past
is more infinite than present or future, it
enlarges each day by the amount that
the others decrease. It expands

like my understanding of my mother, those houses
were cleaner than her own, some had views
that made city lights mirror stars. Even so
she didn't mind dirt, the dust
so much like ashes of loved ones.

SHE'S FLORIDA MISSOURI BUT SHE WAS BORN IN VALHERMOSA AND LIVES IN OHIO

My mother's named for places, not Sandusky
that has wild hair soliciting the moon like blue-black
clouds touring. Not Lorain with ways too benevolent
for lay life. Ashtabula comes closer, southern,
evangelical and accented, her feet wide as yams.

She's Florida Missouri, a railroad, sturdy boxcars
without life of their own, filled and refilled with
what no one can carry.

You just can't call somebody Ravenna who's going
to have to wash another woman's bras and panties, who's
going to wear elbow-length dishwater to formal gigs,
who's going to have to work with her hands, folding and
shuffling them in prayer.

SHE DID MY HAIR OUTSIDE, THE WASH
A TENT AROUND US

Right over left, left over right, Mama
disciplines braids. The Hair Rep melting
on her fingers irrigates my corn rows.
She sings *don't let this harvest pass you by.*
I struggle to stay a child but I hear her.
I'm between her knees and see myself as
Papa's overalls coming through the wringer
Jewish flat bread. The Jewess is downstairs.
Logic postulated convergence of our lives. Her songs
burn me too, my hair steams while the comb reheats.

Papa's name is Abednego. He works with rubber.
He has become as waterproof as his tires. Baptism
washes off him. He and the Jewess are in the
same boat; too bad it's fire next time. I'm on
the masthead. I'm in his wallet, on the Jewess'
polished piano top. Framed. The trip through the
wringer superimposes me on sensitive paper. Caring
paper. Jew-skin paper on which you write love and
kisses. Then you send it through the wringer without
letting go. Special delivery. Mama's fingers
the woof of my braids. Mooring. The same boat.
Hair Rep river. Drifting to roots. Kinky. Nappy.
Textured. Mama's blind and finds her way to
me, rocking the boat, rocking me in an autistic
way that saves.

THE HEALING AND CLOROX

There's no mistaking that level of cleanliness,
no other way to attain it. I was told the Clorox
would eat my skin, eat my insides, treat my body
like any other dirt.

Wind-whipped dungarees assumed our heaviness when
we put them on. I wanted the voile and eyelet gown
to still float when Mama wore it, not wrinkle or
sag like our couch. The mattresses too. We made
graves when we slept and walked.

It really could have passed for beverage but for
the smell that lifts me out of myself, reverses
my dive till I break free of my reflection and
vanity forever, till I flutter like gauze soaking
up sunshine, like truce, and approach an infinite

thinning; my mother doesn't have to reach deeply
within me to find her lost laughter.

TO BUCKWHEAT AND OTHER PICKANINNIES

Mammy (you don't mean to call her that but it's
contagious) put all those bows in your head to
decorate you the way life
probably won't. She put them there while
she dreamt of kites, that's for damn sure,
since not a single moment wasn't given over
to kites that soared (thank God) yet were
tethered (thank God) to her waist which is
the version of a teat meaningful to a kite.

Don't take with you, Buckwheat, a picture
of Mammy with a corn broom yoking her
shoulders, potatoes in her hands like an
abortionist's by-products; a little respect
and that rag on her head would make her an
official swami. Bluets garnish her toes that
splay and grip like fingers, never having been
cloistered in shoes. If all her walking
were in a straight line, she'd be in Canada
after which there's only heaven but you don't
know either place, Buckwheat. The shoes you shine
outshine you and the coins tossed like peanuts
bring out the Judas in you (I envy how it's out
of your system). Now it's just a matter of
whom to betray first.

Some people have you (or your brother Farina)
for breakfast, drown you in milk, a shower
of cinnamon, rusty rain, a grainy web of sugar.
What did they know of the comfort of a flour
sack, those who designed your costume for
The Little Rascals, seeking a match for the
discomfort assumed you felt wearing your skin?

Mammy and those red flags marking quarantine
in your head. That bouquet of bleeding
flowers will be rejected at the door, you
will go stag (as usual) to the opera, nothing
keeps you from the opera, the one place that
resembles your reality, someone singing their
pain and tragedy in a language the audience doesn't
understand (Hear that applause? They want more)
despite the interpreters: those ribbons, crash
sites. Look at the kite strings of your hair
tied into knots like balls and chains.

THE PARTY TO WHICH WOLVES ARE INVITED

I'm five years old.
My parents tell me I'll turn into a boy
if I kiss my elbow.
(I have a moustache because I almost
succeeded).

I like to hear them at night
trying to kiss their own elbows
and turn into each other,
she thinking to show him
what a husband should be,
he intending to teach her
a thing or two about wives.

When the moon gets full of itself
my parents do not make love.
We live in an attic. We make do.

The lightning flashes as night is executed.

I'd rather kiss toads.

Stormtrooping thunder arrives. Anne is doomed.

See Anne. See Anne run. Run, Anne, run to
Burundi, 95 of every 100 adults (and all of the
children) can't read or write or draw swastikas.

I knew it; I'm dreaming I lift violets to her nose.
She pots the scent in beer steins.

I go to summer camp in a Radio Flyer wagon.
I lift the violets to her nose. I've botched my
memory. I kiss her elbow. She's in my cabin.
She can't swim either. We kiss toads in the swamp.

The graves are muddy. The rain mistakes them for
bathtubs. The toads turn into paterollers, sell
us. From the frying pan, Anne, into the fire.
My parents do not make love. The moon is full of
itself. Look at that yellow skin; bet my bottom
dollar the baby will be mulatto. No one's on bottom,
no one's on top, my parents do not make love.
Runagate, runagate. Keep moving. Women and children
first. Every man for himself. Kiss the blood off my
elbow, please. I'm homesick. I send letters
with no return address. I don't know where I
am, where the attic is. All I know is that I smell
violets. I must be near the woods. Near wolves.
They have no elbows. I can kiss them all
day long and they won't turn into something else.

Now I want my parents to step out and yell
surprise. Otherwise, anything that moves
is a wolf.

THE MANDATORY KISS

Sometimes your lover means to swallow you,
your surname disappearing into his history.
He inhales more deeply than you, pulling the air
to the bottom of himself, inflating his shadow.
The rhythm of his breathing is so intense you dance
to it. When you kiss him, you breathe like
another shadow.

It's a simple change of address, your mail and
liabilities rerouted. Like divers with one tank,
you could take turns and both ascend; you'd lose only
the pleasure, would make the kiss mandatory.

I just hope Judas got more than he paid for, the
Savior's skin under his lips, dimpling then springing
back like reciprocation.

for Jesse Wennik

REDBONES AS NOTHING SPECIAL

It is 1960 and a crowd is
at Redbones. There is a jukebox, don't
know why I didn't say so before.
The music, the talk, the cuesticks
are all percussion. The rhythm
inculcates that something is stirring
underground, a funky subway.
It can be so dark and dusky in there
teeth, eyes, red lips seem to have come
unescorted. And this is nice.
All the rear ends at Redbones are convex.
This too is nice.

While the good deacons, the fine sisters
boycott W. T. Grant's, they can still
go to Redbones' booths that become pulpits
when the deacons and sisters commence the
laying on of hands. I like the men with
gold teeth, I like to call them paydirt.
The Alabama clay slowdragging
with bicuspids and incisors.

THE WHORE ON PROSPECT AVENUE

The specialty shops moved to the suburbs
leaving discount stores and record shops
whose gaudy merchandise makes the whores
a better buy for the money.

As one bends to tend a run, she reveals
her legs have curtsied.

I want to let her know I understand even
though she's not between the alley and the
bus stop seeking understanding. My
compassion pours unsolicited from the
vending machine she doesn't kick for not
dispensing cigarettes.

The Bible that will be in her room tonight
is neither threat nor comfort, just
landscaping as is my presence.

Across the street is the Mamselle Modeling
Agency where the director handled my breasts
because I walked in without a portfolio or
an appointment or parental consent, off the
street like dust and the smells of urine
Rorschached on concrete.

The whore wears gold lassos in her ears.
Sometimes she doesn't take her makeup off till
the next day when she's about to reapply it.
Whatever she shows isn't her real face, she
keeps something sacred.

A STRADIVARIUS IN DIEN BIEN PHU

Today blackbirds lend their wings to French
loaves rescued from ovens. All the obituary
notices begin with O, with surprise. Not much
can compensate for the missing Stradivarius. Why
did the lieutenant take it to Dien Bien Phu?

On my way to school, celibate Jesus' wives return,
their habits stiff sympathy cards. The convent is
my shortcut in sour weather. The patina of Mary
is the only thing inside the color of money.
Theirs are the only white faces on Chapelside Road.

Mrs. Johnson, the lieutenant's wife who wants to
tell them her husband is missing in action too, is
the Avon Lady supplying free samples to the site that
because of them will be a shrine to another Lady.

I know the signs of unhappy marriages.
Sister Margaret's breath sometimes smells of Cotillion
cologne. A Stradivarius pregnant with Mozart decomposes.

FAITH IN A GLASS

Faith keeps chopsticks the envy of
crippled men. Disembodied birds flit
through Cantonese dishes.

Earthquakes are the way the faithful dig
mass graves. The trembling is the grief,
the heaving shoulders. A sudden squall

of leaves is the flight of one-winged
butterflies because faith tells me this
is possible. What can I tell faith?

So I do not dig new wells. My dry cough
hacks away until something I didn't know
was within loosens. I do not verify

sunrise with a glance out the window.
I rely on a lightening of spirit.
My faith is in the bedside glass where

teeth would be if I had none. When I thirst
at those hours that both hunger and thirst
usually recede, faith moves down my throat,

prickly water. I look for signs of lost faith
in my urine. Some cities smell of that loss.
Otherwise priestly men confess before urinals.

Some never leave, everlasting streams of faith
deepening the red of bricks into Negro complexions.
And it looks so much like beer that you know

aspirations have fermented, mother of vinegar has
provided the nurturing. My dead mother is faith.
The one in Ohio still wears pink lipstick though

she's too brown for it. She buttons her coat to
the top expecting chill winds from the Arctic to
dip south any season. That is the kind of faith

left. The other, the missing, used to shatter
the glass it sinks in.

THE TATTOO

He had a blonde woman on his chest and he
was in prison. Just her head and it
was tilted so that she could look up at
his chin, the cliff just jumped off.

She's the glossy cover superimposed on
the table, the vinyl Chrysler seat,
wherever she lies.

A convict improvising isn't new. A black man
made a convict by the blonde woman on his chest
isn't new. Decapitations aren't new. Nothing
this man did is new. He didn't mean to be
a copy cat.

He wore her like a designer label. With her on
you could call him revealed but not naked.
She masked his heart. She kept it from hungry
others, even the starving self.

It was like she was being born right from
his rib cage. It was like rereading Genesis.
He was just a dark transitory cocoon.
It was like he just wanted to boast
about what he could produce
besides excrement.

VICIOUS CIRCLES IN THE TRENCHES

Here's what happened when I broke a promise made
to Mama on her deathbed: I stacked all the plates in
the middle of the room. I put on my coat and stood
by the door. I thought about who was not going
to enter, the president, an angel, my father.
His return was not the broken promise.
I thought about how I would feel learning Mama
had died while I stood still. So I set the plates
spinning. I put my finger on them like a phonograph
needle and heard the music of a life falling apart.
Here's what I'll really feel about dying: proud
of finishing, just once, something started.
The plates broke in round pieces. I set them spinning.
I recited all the common prayers (only whores are more
common) then I set them spinning. I ran for my life
and could not get elected. I set it spinning. Mama and
Daddy used to dance. I set them spinning in my head, they
waltzed right out and left me spinning. Because I had on
a trench coat, I went to the trenches and laid by my mother,
a revolving skeleton key gouging me while trying to open me.
It's hard to bandage your life with bones.

WEIGHING THE SINS OF THE WORLD

If you have Mantovani on you don't even feel
the weight. The elevator is a padded cradle.
Your vision is shallow yet clear so you direct
traffic from the signpost between right and wrong.
No job could be easier. You're a winner.

Jazz is the consolation prize, it smokes, it
heaves, it pa-pa-pants, pa-pa-pants. Trellises
of notes climb the walls. And when the horn's
bell melts, use Van Gogh's ear, trumpet sunflowers
that become stars withstanding the storms of breath
summoned up from behind the belly button, the cork
in the dike. Mantovani is one brushstroke in this
composition, lost in a swirl. Either abandon
barrettes and get anchors or let the wind from the man
shape your long hair into red saxophones. This is
the second coming, his second wind; keep playing, man,
keep playing. Play me a trail of tears for the Cherokee
nation. Play me a raft for a runaway slave. Play me
a spectre of myself. Hook the sax around my arm
like handcuffs; I have no Mantovani. I'm guilty.

Back at the ranch, it's a square-dance.
The fiddle is the city of screeching brakes.
Jazz is the hitchhiker left behind. A pretty
little thing climbs into the cab of a truck hauling
saxophone caskets. (Put a horn in a case and you
kill it.) Anyway, the talk here is of consumption.
Being isolated from priests. Having
to cough up blood for communion. Then finally
getting the Eucharist and its the wrong blood type.
It's a fatal transfusion. And that's jazz.
That's the need to keep pumping in jazz intravenously
after draining yourself to play it.

When I met my husband I told him I was interested only
in musicians. He showed me his penile saxophone and
said "What do you think I am?" And I said "that's cool"
so as to appear unaffected. Really, he was hot.

Okay, so you know why my bedroom spins, the walls
centrifugally kept from collapsing. The circular fence
of sound will be with me as long as I'm willing to be dizzy.

If you have Mantovani and you're on the
signpost, you can't help me get where I'm already
going. You're like the crucifix that may be on
the bedroom wall, the whir makes it vanish into
the motion. Stop and the cross clarifies and
I see both of you pointing to the four deadends
of the earth.

A saxophone was taken off the cross, had to play
itself three days before the notes lowered
to audibility.

THE SIN WASHING GIMMICK

Jesus' fame as a sin washer spread because
he washed sins for free. You didn't have to supply
your own soap which was useless anyway in removing
pigment. Blood sins were his
specialty. When Jesus was done, you
couldn't tell who had killed, who had been
killed. We didn't mind giving up rainbows.

My sins are white as snow now and lovely.
I didn't argue about something maybe being
whiter, Bangor, Maine, South Boston. Snow
represents white well. White is so easy to
represent. Sometimes a mirage will do.

On Father's Day, a corsage of clean sins looks
elegant on my sleeve. They petal, flake like
fully cooked haddock. I am tempted to eat them
so I know they are sins. Had Jesus eaten them
instead of being wounded by them, he would have
died anyway.

Being clean is paramount as any good mother
knows. The daily washing of underwear in case
of accident so that healing can begin with a
doctor's willing touch. Bottled Jesus is the
Clorox that whitens old sheets, makes the Klan
a brotherhood of saints.

The goal is becoming white not to stop being
sin. Not to deny identity. A diamond, for
instance, whitened coal, is ruthless in the
cutting of glass.

BOTANICAL FANATICISM

My ancestors weren't hippies, cotton
precluded fascination with flowers.
I don't remember communes, I remember
ghettos. The riots were real, not
products of hallucinogens. Free love had
been at Redbones since black unemployment
and credit saturation.

The white women my mother cleaned
for didn't notice she had changed. I guess
it was a small event, a resurrected African
jumping out the gap in her front teeth. I
guess it looked like a cockroach; that's
what she was supposed to have, not dignity.

My mother just couldn't get excited
about the Beatles, those mops she swilled
in ammonia everyday on their heads. Besides,
she didn't work like a dog but like a woman;
they aren't the same. The hair was growing long
for the same reasons Pinocchio's nose did.

I can think only of a lesbian draping
crepe paper chains over my head to make a
black Rapunzel possible; that's how a white
woman tried to lift my burdens. At the time
I didn't reject her for being lesbian or
white but for both burdens. That was when
I didn't want Ivory soap to be what
cleaned me, made me presentable to society.
All the suds I'd seen were white, they still
are but who cares? I'm more interested in
how soap dwindles in my hand, under the faucet.

I'm old enough to remember blocks
of ice, old enough or poor enough.
I remember chipping away at it, broken
glass all over the floor. Later in the
riots, the broken glass of looting tattled
how desperate people were to keep cool.

There are roses now in my mother's yard.
Sometimes she cuts them, sets them in Pepsi
bottles throughout her rooms. She is,
I admit, being sentimental. Looting her
heart. My father who planted them is gone.
That mop in the corner
is his cane growing roots.

SUNRISE COMES TO SECOND AVENUE

Daylight announces
the start of a day six hours old.

We all have thankless
jobs to do. Consider

the devotion of fishes singing
hymns without voices.

The clock's hands searching
for the lost face, a place

for the Eucharist. The man
bedded down on the roadway,

the asphalt pope out of bread,
breath and blessings.

The streetcleaner
sweeping up confessions.

ASCENSION

Indians do not fear
heights. Mounting
scaffolding is
no power struggle
with God.

They are not afraid
of grabbing handfuls
of nothing. Aviators
passing through the
same clouds
report turbulence.

The drawbridges
they transcend stymie
ordinary motorists
who see morgue tablets
without commandments,
tombstones.

Although we think the top
is lonely, how can it be
when up there they see
everything, how big the
world is, how full.

God
has to be an
Indian.

Words like *Sioux*,
Comanche fuse
like the Host
with the tongue.

A GODIVA

Myself, I always thought it
a throwback revealing primate roots
I'd as soon forget. Oh but what

would I do without that stuff
softer than a hand, a spool
unwound on my head and gold
already, before

the weaver comes with that talent
I share; my one-word name
rivals the best of them:
Rumplestiltskin, God.

My calling came and I went public as
a hedge on horseback in Coventry, the
sun fermenting the color of my hair
into grog that will not

lay wasted. *Eat, drink, be merry*
those aren't nude words. I put it all
on the table for surgery, not feast.
I want to be cut through to my

black woman's heart. She had one
in 1057 as well as a continent
that had not been reconciled nor
clothed. Breasts hanging as fruit

should, unpicked sculpture on a
tree, museum pieces. She is
something good for you that is not
medicine. And I

am her transmitted, no longer
literal, needful of reasons
to take off clothes that don't explain
living, and distort everything God

gave us, while trying to be
metaphors for the gifts. If I succeed
there is a tax that will die. I ride
like a morbid Midas, my lips

and fingers coax their love objects
into the most golden silence of them all.
The usual death rider got time off
for good behavior. I just worry

that I might like this, that I'll take
my heart out of the black woman and
put it in a dead thing.

STAKING TERRITORY

My husband gives up and goes to bed without
me, leaving the windows, the only paintings we
hung, to myself. At night, I look out and see
endlessness that makes me crave the finitude that
really is mine. The best boxers train by punching
through plate glass.

My husband is graying at the temples, turning into
concrete, giving me a more solid foundation for
worship. At St. Paul's, the cracked walls testify
that a growing holiness is splitting the seams.
The lone dollar in the collection plate lacks a means
to amplify its testimony.

Men walk down the boulevard carrying sides of beef.
No one is without an escort. The times do not permit
private ventures. The roadway's after-rainfall sheen
says slick operation, scam, hustle. Only snakes
have tongues as long as this road. The sole of a big
inconsiderate shoe.

The bus stop is a metal lollipop. Accepting
this candy from an estranged city is wrong.
Just in time the bus comes, a metal loaf, and
not the chariot. The night is a great map, takes
you to any dark place you want to go.